LET'S FIND OUT! *RELIGION*

CHRISTIANITY

LYNNAE D. STEINBERG

Britannica®
Educational Publishing

IN ASSOCIATION WITH

ROSEN
EDUCATIONAL SERVICES

Published in 2019 by Britannica Educational Publishing (a trademark of Encyclopædia Britannica, Inc.) in association with The Rosen Publishing Group, Inc.
29 East 21st Street, New York, NY 10010

Distributed exclusively by Rosen Publishing.
To see additional Britannica Educational Publishing titles, go to rosenpublishing.com.

First Edition

Britannica Educational Publishing
J.E. Luebering: Executive Director, Core Editorial
Mary Rose McCudden: Editor, Britannica Student Encyclopedia

Rosen Publishing
Jacob R. Steinberg: Editor
Nicole Russo-Duca: Series Designer and Book Layout
Cindy Reiman: Photography Manager
Sherri Jackson: Photo Researcher

Library of Congress Cataloging-in-Publication Data

Names: Steinberg, Lynnae D., 1957– author.
Title: Christianity / Lynnae D. Steinberg.
Description: First edition. | New York : Britannica Educational Publishing, in Association with Rosen Educational Services, 2019. | Series: Let's find out! Religion | Includes bibliographical references and index. | Audience: Grades 1–5.
Identifiers: LCCN 2018014135 | ISBN 9781508106845 (library bound) | ISBN 9781508107156 (pbk.) | ISBN 9781508107262 (6 pack)
Subjects: LCSH: Christianity—Juvenile literature.
Classification: LCC BR125.5 .S74 2018 | DDC 230—dc23
LC record available at https://lccn.loc.gov/2018014135

Manufactured in the United States of America

Photo credits: Cover and interior pages background vvoe/Shutterstock.com; p. 4 © Encyclopædia Britannica, Inc.; p. 5 Renata Sedmakova/Shutterstock.com; p. 6 © Photos.com/Jupiterimages; p. 7 Brand X Pictures /Stockbyte/Getty Images; p. 8 Andreas Solaro/AFP/Getty Images; p. 9 James L. Amos/National Geographic Image Collection/Getty Images; p. 10 © Graphic House/Encyclopædia Britannica, Inc.; p. 11 Sirtravelalot /Shutterstock.com; p. 12 © Andy Rhodes/Fotolia; p. 13 Alexander Gatsenko/Shutterstock.com; p. 14 Renata Sedmakova/Shutterstock.com; p. 15 Godong/robertharding/Getty Images; p. 16 Geography Photos/Universal Images Group/Getty Images; pp. 17, 19 © Photos.com/Jupiterimages; pp. 18, 20 Photos.com/Thinkstock; p. 21 Prisma Archivo/Alamy Stock Photo; p. 22 Egbert van Heemskerk the Elder/Getty Images; p. 23 Patrick Bernard /AFP/Getty Images; p. 24 Steve Heap/Shutterstock.com; pp. 25, 29 © AP Images; p. 26 The AGE/Fairfax Media /Getty Images; p. 27 Portland Press Herald/Getty Images; p. 28 Filippo Monteforte/AFP/Getty Images.

CONTENTS

WHAT IS CHRISTIANITY?

With some two billion followers, Christianity is the most widespread religion in the world. Like Islam and Judaism, Christianity is **monotheistic**. It teaches that

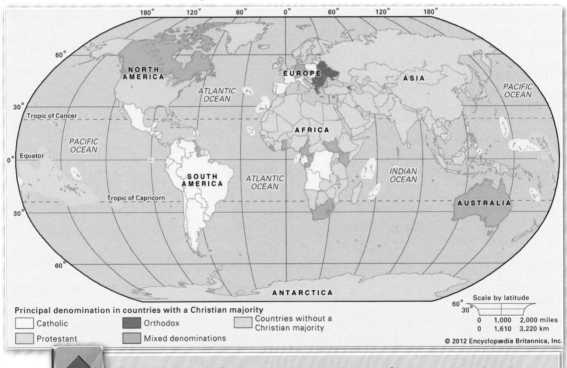

Principal denomination in countries with a Christian majority

Catholic	Orthodox	Countries without a Christian majority
Protestant	Mixed denominations	

Scale by latitude

© 2012 Encyclopædia Britannica, Inc.

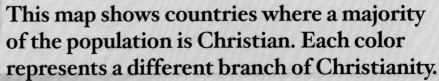

This map shows countries where a majority of the population is Christian. Each color represents a different branch of Christianity.

VOCABULARY

Monotheistic religions teach the belief that there is only one God, rather than many gods or none at all.

there is only one God and that God created the world.

Christianity is based on the life, death, and teachings of Jesus of Nazareth, who lived long ago in the Middle East. Christians believe that Jesus is the Christ, or chosen one, whom God sent to the world to save people. Central to Christianity is love for God above all things. Christianity also tells people to love one another and to be forgiving, humble, and kind.

Christianity has three main branches—Roman Catholicism, Eastern Orthodoxy, and Protestantism. Despite these different branches, Christians see themselves as one worldwide community.

Christians believe that Jesus was sent by God to save humanity.

BELIEFS AND PRACTICES

Christians believe that Jesus is the son of God. He was sent to Earth, where he had to suffer, die, and be resurrected to make up for people's sins. Christians view Jesus's new life after death as hope that they, too, may be granted everlasting life. Christians also believe in the Trinity. The Trinity, which means the three, is the idea that three figures are united in one God: God the Father, God the Son (Jesus), and God the Holy Spirit.

This fifteenth-century painting shows Jesus's resurrection. Christians believe they, too, will have everlasting life.

In church, Christians pray, sing, and listen to Bible readings and a sermon—a talk given by a priest or a minister.

The Holy Spirit is thought of as a helper sent to guide and teach people.

Christians gather together to worship in churches. Sunday is the most common day of worship. Services usually involve singing, prayer, Bible readings, and a sermon.

COMPARE AND CONTRAST

How are the three figures of the Trinity different? What do they have in common?

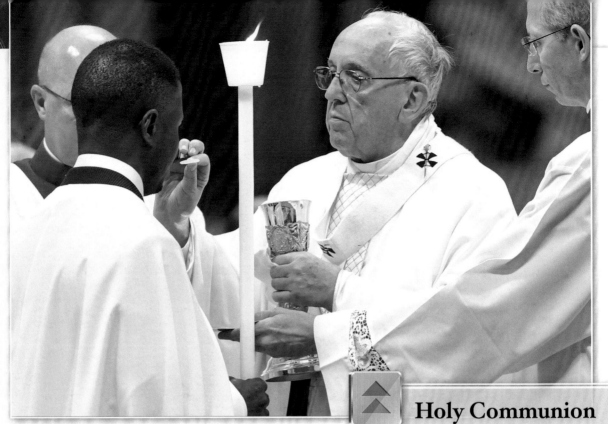

Holy Communion is an important part of the Roman Catholic service called a Mass.

In many churches, services include a ceremony called Holy Communion (or the Eucharist). In the Bible, Jesus gathered his followers together for a meal, known as the Last Supper. Jesus told them that his death was necessary because it would make a new bond between God and people. Jesus took bread and wine, blessed them, and shared them with his followers.

In the Communion ceremony, Christians eat a special piece of bread and, in some churches, drink a sip of wine or grape juice. In many Christian churches, children make their first Holy Communion when they are about seven years old.

Baptism is also an important ritual for Christians. It involves the spiritual cleansing of sins and acceptance into God's church. People of any age may be baptized, though in many Christian churches, people are baptized as infants. During baptism, a person may be sprinkled with water or immersed completely under water.

A father holds his infant during a baptism ceremony.

THE BIBLE

The Bible is the sacred text of Christianity. It is made up of two main parts: the Old Testament and the New Testament. The Bible was written by many different authors over many hundreds of years. The Old Testament describes how God made a covenant, or agreement, with the people of Israel and chose them to be a special people. The Old Testament also contains the Ten Commandments, laws which say there is one God and describe how to treat others. For example, they forbid stealing, killing, or lying.

After Jesus's death, Christians created the

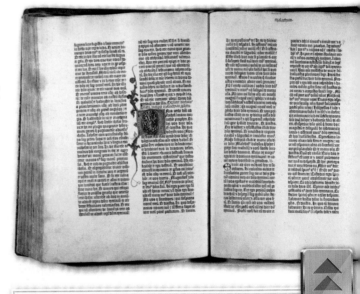

This copy of the Bible was printed in about 1455 CE by a man named Johannes Gutenberg in Germany.

As part of Christian worship services, a religious leader, such as a priest or a minister, reads aloud from the Bible.

New Testament to spread the message of Jesus. Four books, called the Gospels, tell about Jesus's life and teachings. The Acts of the Apostles tell about the early history of the church

COMPARE AND CONTRAST

Both Christians and Jews believe in the Old Testament, or Hebrew Bible. Can you think of other similarities between Christianity and Judaism?

and its messengers, or apostles, after Jesus's death. The Epistles are letters of advice and instruction. And finally, the Book of Revelation describes the end of the world.

JESUS'S LIFE

Christians believe that Jesus was the Messiah—a savior sent to save people from sin. The word "Christ" comes from *Khristos*, the Greek word for Messiah. According to the Bible, a woman named Mary gave birth to Jesus in about 6 BCE in Bethlehem, a city in the Middle Eastern region of Palestine. Mary and her husband, Joseph, were Jews from Nazareth, and that is where Jesus grew up.

A stained glass window in a church shows Mary holding a newborn Jesus as her husband, Joseph, watches over them.

Little is known of Jesus's youth. There is a story that tells of Jesus, even at a young age, showing interest in religion. It says he spoke with Jewish leaders about faith. Jesus's father on Earth was a carpenter. Many people believe that Jesus followed in his father's footsteps and was also a carpenter as a young man.

THINK ABOUT IT

There are few records about Jesus's life as a child, but there are more about his life as an adult. What is the value of having historical records?

Today, Nazareth is a city in the Middle Eastern country of Israel. Many devout Christians visit holy sites in Nazareth.

Jesus began preaching when he was about thirty years old. He gathered a group of twelve followers, called the Apostles, who helped him spread his message. Many of Jesus's teachings grew out of Judaism. He taught people to honor God and live peaceful, moral lives so they could enter Heaven. He often taught by using parables to explain his message.

Jesus attracted many followers, but not everyone liked his teachings. Jesus welcomed all types of people, even those whom Jewish religious leaders considered to be sinners. Some religious leaders thought that Jesus's

Jesus had twelve close followers, the Apostles, who listened to and helped spread his teachings. Here they eat with Jesus shortly before his death.

COMPARE AND CONTRAST

Think of other peaceful figures, such as Martin Luther King, Jr., who faced opposition because of their ideas. What do they have in common with Jesus? What makes their stories different?

Christians believe Jesus died for their sins, so the image of Jesus nailed to a cross is a common Christian symbol.

teaching was wrong and that it was leading people astray. Others feared that he might start a political uprising, and that this would lead to great trouble. The leaders decided to have Jesus put to death. Jesus was crucified, or nailed to a cross, and died. The Bible tells of Jesus's resurrection and his return to heaven.

THE SPREAD OF CHRISTIANITY

For many years, Jesus's followers continued to practice religion the same way as Jews, except they believed Jesus was a savior sent from God. To help spread Jesus's teachings, some early Christians wrote about him. Writings by four men—Matthew, Mark, Luke and John—tell of Jesus's life and teachings. These writings now make up the Gospels of the New Testament. Some of Jesus's followers became **missionaries**

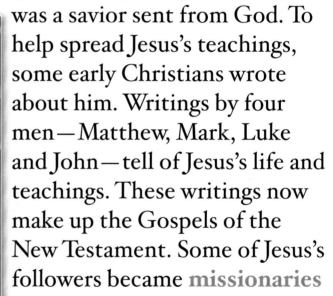

An English church painting shows Matthew, one of the four saints whose writings make up the Gospels of the New Testament.

and moved to other lands. The most important missionary was a man named Paul. Jesus and his earliest followers preached only to the Jewish community, but Paul spread Jesus's teachings to those who were not Jewish. As the message of Jesus's teaching spread, Christianity was born.

In the early days of Christianity, life was difficult and even dangerous for Christians. The Roman Empire controlled the region, and the government did not approve of the new religion.

Paul the Apostle is shown preaching to a group of Athenians. He was the first Christian missionary to spread Jesus's teachings to non-Jews.

When the Roman emperor Constantine became a Christian in 312 CE, the religion spread throughout the Roman Empire quickly.

A Roman emperor converted to Christianity in 312 CE, however. That helped create acceptance of Christianity. By the end of the 300s CE, Christianity was the Roman Empire's official religion.

Christianity continued to grow during the Middle Ages, a period from about the year 500 CE to about 1500 CE. The leaders of the Christian church became powerful and wealthy, and the church grew to become the most powerful cultural force in Europe.

In 1095 CE Pope Urban II called on members of the church to spread Christianity in a series of wars called the Crusades.

As Christianity grew, it could not remain unified. In 1054 CE the Eastern church at Constantinople separated from the Western church in Rome because of differences in beliefs and practices. This split created the Eastern Orthodox churches and the Roman Catholic Church.

COMPARE AND CONTRAST

Compare and contrast the role of a religious leader with that of a nonreligious leader, such as a president or a king.

LATER BRANCHES

In the early 1500s almost everyone in western and central Europe was Roman Catholic, and the church was very powerful. A German priest named Martin Luther began to question certain religious

THINK ABOUT IT

Many groups in history have punished people who did not think the same way that they did. Does this still happen today? If so, how can we change that?

Meant to change some Catholic practices, Martin Luther's teachings caused a reform movement known as the Reformation.

practices of Catholicism. He did not agree with the amount of power and wealth held by the church. Luther also disagreed with many of the rituals used in the church.

Luther's criticism helped bring about the religious revolution known as the Reformation. As a result of the Reformation, the first Protestant

In the Inquisition, people who opposed the Catholic Church were judged in public ceremonies.

churches were founded. The Roman Catholic Church tried to stop the spread of Protestantism with its own movement, the Counter-Reformation. Members of a religious order known as the Jesuits spread Roman Catholicism through their teaching and missionary work. A Catholic court system called the Inquisition punished people who disobeyed church teachings.

Quakers were just one of the many Protestant denominations who sought greater religious freedom in North America during the colonial era.

By the mid-1600s Europe was mostly divided into Protestant and Catholic regions. Most of these divisions have remained in place. In the 1600s the settlers of the British colonies brought Protestantism to North America. With more than 500 million followers today, Protestantism is the second largest branch of Christianity. It is divided into many different denominations including the Lutheran, Baptist, Methodist, and Quaker churches.

Although many Protestant churches have different beliefs, all Protestants reject Roman Catholicism and the power of its leader, the pope. They base their beliefs on the Christian Bible. Most believe that getting to heaven requires only faith in God, not any specific actions. They think that each believer, not just priests, can spread God's teachings.

An Anglican priest leads a prayer service. Anglicanism is a Protestant branch but follows some Catholic practices.

HOLIDAYS

Three of the most important days of the year for Christians are Christmas, Epiphany, and Easter. Christmas celebrates the birth of Jesus. The day and year of his birth are not certain. Roman Catholics and Protestants celebrate Christmas on December 25, and the Eastern Orthodox church celebrates on January 6. Many traditions from

Decorating a tree, sharing a festive meal, and exchanging gifts are popular ways to celebrate Christmas.

around the world are tied to this festive holiday, such as decorating a Christmas tree and exchanging gifts.

Another important holiday is Epiphany. The word "epiphany" means "appearance." In the Eastern churches, Epiphany mainly celebrates Jesus's baptism. In the Western church, Christians celebrate Epiphany as the day that the three Wise Men, or Magi, visited the baby Jesus with gifts. For this reason, Epiphany is sometimes called Three Kings Day. The evening before Epiphany, called Twelfth Night, is celebrated in many European countries.

THINK ABOUT IT

Many families celebrate Christmas in ways that reflect their cultural roots. Why do you think people celebrate Christmas in different ways?

Some cities have parades and public celebrations on Epiphany.

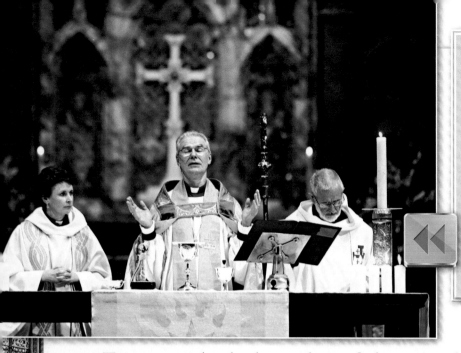

Easter is the holiest day of the year for Christians. It celebrates their belief in the resurrection of Jesus Christ. A celebration of new life, Easter occurs in the spring.

In many churches, Easter follows a period of prayer and fasting called Lent. Lent is observed in memory of the forty days Jesus is said to have fasted in the desert. In Roman Catholic and Protestant churches, Lent begins with Ash Wednesday. This day gets its name from the practice of putting ashes on the foreheads of the faithful as a symbol of the season. During Lent, many Christians fast, or go without regular meals, on certain days. Some

THINK ABOUT IT

Even though it was sad, the day that Jesus died was named Good Friday. Why do you think it has that name?

Christians "fast" during Lent by giving up something that they enjoy, such as a favorite food or a fun activity.

The week before Easter is known as Holy Week. During this week, Christians remember the events leading up to Jesus's death. The day on which he was crucified is Good Friday.

In celebration of new life, children decorate eggs and are greeted on Easter morning with baskets of goodies left by the Easter Bunny.

CHRISTIANITY TODAY

Pope Francis is the current leader of the Roman Catholic Church. He is trying to make Catholicism more accepting and open.

Christian missionaries have spread their religion throughout much of the world. Christian churches in Africa and Latin America have become important centers of Christianity. In 2013 a priest from Argentina was named pope of the Roman Catholic Church. The pope is the leader of the church throughout the

world. Pope Francis is known for his efforts to revitalize the Roman Catholic Church and make it more welcoming.

Today Christianity is the most popular religion in the United States. About 70 percent of the US population is some denomination of Christian. Some Christian churches have large congregations, with memberships numbering in the thousands. Today, many Christian churches use the Internet and television to spread their messages and connect with younger worshippers.

Christians gather in a large church to hear a famous pastor. Some church services are shown on television or the Internet.

GLOSSARY

carpenter A worker who builds or repairs wooden structures.

commandment A rule to follow.

disobeyed Refused or failed to obey.

empire A large territory or a number of territories or peoples under one ruler with total authority.

faith Religious belief.

forgiving Inclined or ready to forgive.

Gospel One of the first four New Testament books telling of the life, death, and resurrection of Jesus Christ.

humble Modest; not proud or bold.

Jesuits An all-male religious order within the Roman Catholic Church, founded in 1534.

Middle East The region around the southern and eastern shores of the Mediterranean Sea.

minister A leader of a group of worshippers, especially within a Protestant church.

moral Guided by right behavior.

Nazareth Town of ancient Palestine in central Galilee; now a city in northern Israel.

opposition Disagreement with someone or something.

parable A short simple story illustrating a moral or spiritual truth.

priest A religious leader of the Roman Catholic Church.

region An area.

resurrected Raised from the dead; brought back to life.

savior A person that saves from danger or destruction.

sermon A talk that teaches a lesson and is given by a priest or a minister.

unified Grouped together as a whole.

uprising An act or instance of fighting against authority.

FOR MORE INFORMATION

Books

Furgang, Kathy. *Pope Francis: Priest of the People* (Junior Biographies). New York, NY: Enslow Publishing, 2017.

Goodings, Christina, and Maria Royse. *Who Is Jesus?* Oxford, UK: Lion Children's, 2016.

Marsico, Katie. *Christianity*. Ann Arbor, MI: Cherry Lake Publishing, 2017.

Owen, Ruth. *Handmade Christmas Crafts*. New York, NY: Gareth Stevens Publishing, 2017.

Ponto, Joanna. *Easter* (Story of Our Holidays). New York, NY: Enslow Publishing, 2016.

Websites

Kids Past
https://kidspast.com/world-history/christianity/

United Religions Initiative
https://uri.org/kids/world-religions/christian-beliefs

World Religions for Kids
https://sites.google.com/site/worldreligionsforkids/christianity

INDEX